BOMBS AT BEDTIME
A Childhood during the Second World War

Chris Rowan Grainger

Published in 2013 by New Generation Publishing

New Generation Publishing, 2 London Wall Buildings, London EC2M 5UU

Copyright © 2013 by Chris Rowan Grainger

First Edition

The author asserts the moral right under the Copyright, Designs and Patents Act 1998 to be identified as the author of this work.

All rights reserved. No part of this publication may be reproduced, stored in a retrieval system, or transmitted in any form or by any means without prior written consent of the author, nor be otherwise circulated in any form of binding or cover other than that in which it is published and without a similar condition being imposed upon the subsequent purchaser.

www.newgeneration-publishing.com

With deep gratitude to Tom Osborne
for his dedicated proof-reading.

To my yet unborn descendants

FOREWORD

Reminiscences can be tedious to those who were not there and absolutely gripping to those who were. But as the events remembered become history they can become more widely interesting. Today it might be quite dull to hear someone going on about the Gulf War, yet, suppose they had been at the Norman Conquest, the reminiscence would have a wide interest and every word would be preserved as if in tissue paper.

I am going to attempt to write some recollections of my childhood which was largely overlaid by the period of the Second World War. It is to be written for my family who succeed me, and to try to tidy up the jumbled rooms which were the first seventeen years of my life.

It is really the story of my three brothers too, but each of them would remember quite different moments, so each tale would be unique.

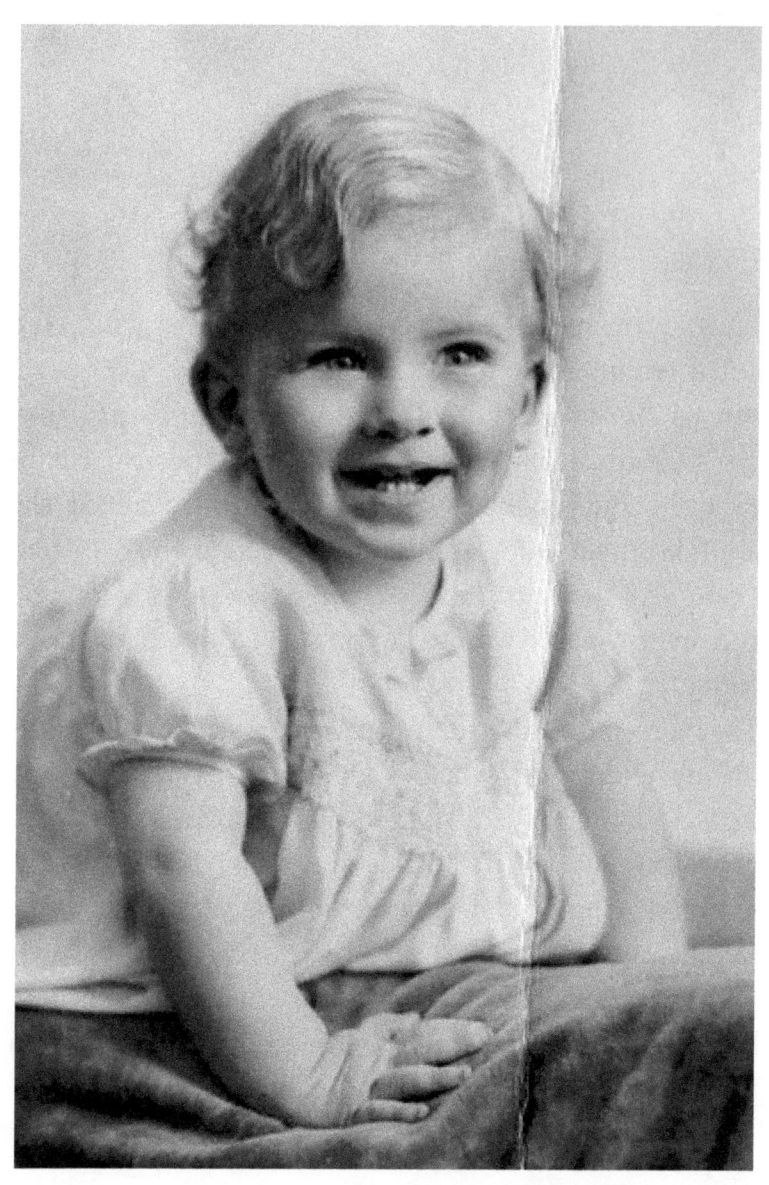

Chris aged one, 1937

ONE

In every family there is a hierarchy according to the order in which people are born. In my family the birth dates of my two elder brothers, Hugh and Stuart, were so close together, 1931 and 1932 that frequently there seemed to be some dispute as to which one was Chief Indian. Hugh was positioned as natural leader but Stuart did not always take kindly to that and there were battles of will, eventually calmed by the realisation that we all only had each other.

When I came along in 1936 the two older boys had already formed an uneasy partnership into which I was sometimes allowed to slot as I progressed out of knitted shawls and the carry-cot. My earliest recollections were of being an inconvenience. Some sort of nanny or girl was put in charge of us. I remember her peering over my cot and being very cross with me about something I didn't understand, when my parents were out. Evidently she was dismissed soon afterwards which must have been a relief to my babyhood. For my mother Lilian to have produced another boy when the whole aim was for a girl was surely very disappointing for her, and I think it took her a little while to be hospitable to me. She was to give birth to twin boys four years later before finally giving up the girl idea for ever.

This was of course before the war started and it was the very end of the time when most middle income families had staff to help in the house. These people were inexpensive to employ but often not trained at all. There were girls to help with the

Leonard Bentall, Grandpa, c.1930

children, girls to clean the house and girls to help in the kitchen with a cook, who was usually older. I don't know how many staff were in and out of our house at that time, but two or more, definitely. The advantages of having people to help are obvious. The lady of the house gave instructions, then went on to do her own thing, whatever that might be. But because numbers of people were involved she had to plan her life with some care. Her energies went into the management of others rather than into manual tasks which were to absorb her strength later on in the war and afterwards, when staff were no longer available. On the other hand the disadvantages of staff are less obvious: they are human, unlike a dishwasher, and are often not ideal for the job. They have to be coaxed and encouraged and reminded and admonished. Having them in the house can make it feel insecure; you never know when they are going to appear in a doorway or be a bit moody and, from a child's point of view, it's unsettling to become used to one girl who seems friendly, only to find you have to adjust to a new one when the other leaves, or is asked to go, for a reason no one would ever dream of explaining.

Our father Geoffrey was an accountant and at this time when we were in Epsom he was working in his wife's family business, the huge department store called Bentalls of Kingston. Leonard Bentall, Grandpa, our mother's father, had created the big emporium, which occupied most of the centre of Kingston upon Thames in Surrey, from a small draper's shop owned by Frank Bentall, his father. Small shop after small shop was bought up until he had a place big enough to match his vision. The store sold everything imaginable from fashion and make-up to pets and building materials. You could have a good meal in the restaurant or buy what you wanted from the food hall and, if you had the money, you could even buy a car in the garage over the road, the size of an aircraft hangar, where people parked before shopping.

The Tudor and Renaissance architecture for Leonard's great shop was influenced by Hampton Court which lies just two miles upstream by the river Thames, so Bentalls was designed with tall, slim windows with round ones above, and high brick chimneys like the famous palace. The nearness of the river made it necessary to install a constant pumping system in the basement to keep the building dry, day and night.

Before the war and for some time afterwards Bentalls was a store of great style, never short of ideas to attract the customers. During the war, when times were hard, Grandpa Bentall invited Bertram Mills Circus to perform in the whole of the lower ground floor – which usually sold tools and household goods – to attract Christmas shoppers. As a small boy I felt the strangeness of a large circus in a big shop – tightrope walkers, jugglers, clowns, acrobats, and a strongman. Even horses cantered around with a girl standing on top.

This Bentalls Boss could be both dictatorial and extremely kind and generous. As young grandchildren we were occasionally invited to Grandpa's office.

The journey took us along beige-carpeted corridors punctuated every so often by oak swing doors. This management part of the store smelt of woollen carpet and typing paper, the typists working in rooms open to the corridor. As we went through each door the rooms became smarter, revealing secretaries of increasing seniority until we came at last to the final door, allowing us into the two offices of the most senior directors. Miss Eggleton, the most special secretary of all, typed Leonard's confidential letters behind her own glass window. I remember once when we were ushered into his office, Grandpa disappeared through a door at the back of his room, looking as though he was running away from us down a private escape route, but soon returning with a Dinky Toy car in a box for each of his grandsons. He seemed fond of us in his distant, all-powerful way, immersed as he was in the constant consideration of his business empire.

As the war progressed, shortages forced everyone to economise and to face up to the real possibility that Hitler's German army might invade Britain at any moment. But before the years of bombs and gunfire, Leonard travelled around in a shiny green and chrome Rolls Royce, driven by his dapper chauffeur called Tapper. As a little boy I caught a brief glimpse of that privileged world which was soon to disappear for ever. One Sunday afternoon I was travelling with Grandpa in the deep, leathery back seat of his big-windowed car when Tapper suddenly sounded the horn. There came an imperious order from his employer:

'Tapper! we never use the horn on Sundays!'

Chris, Stuart, and Hugh with Mother in Devon
Before the outbreak of war in 1939

Tapper had a spiky waxed moustache and wore a uniform of dark grey serge. When not driving the Rolls he did odd jobs around my grandparents' home – Oakwood Court, near Leatherhead. When, as boys, we stayed there and asked him for anything at all, he always said,

'Can't be done.'

I have often thought how different he was from A. A. Milne's 'Jonathan Jo:'

> 'Jonathan Jo
> Has a mouth like an "O"
> And a wheelbarrow full of surprises;
> If you ask for a bat,
> Or for something like that,
> He has got it, whatever the size is.'

Leonard Bentall was an active giver-to-good-causes and started the Steadfast Sea Cadets very successfully in Kingston. There are also stories of his autocracy and sudden changes of mood, but mostly I was too young to experience these. The distance between us was too great.

TWO

Father was not happy working at Bentalls. Perhaps he felt unappreciated, or perhaps, as son-in-law of the owner, he was over critical and expected promotion too quickly, or perhaps there really was a policy of retarding his progress. Anyway, he soon found a new accountancy job in a different department store: Dingles of Plymouth. So in 1938, when I was two, our home was re-established in Devon, a long way from Surrey, at a house called Bradbourne, where we were to stay until bombs drove us out. In the war 'bombed out' became the common expression when your home or place of work was hit.

This was a brief time of security for me, before the time of constant separations began. Sometimes I had Mother and Father to myself. He played his old 'cello of dark wood, and invented with me eccentric games, like making a pretend cardboard radio which we called a wirely box. It only takes a few memories to construct a life-long image of a person and these were a few of the stray mixings of mortar which gave me some bonding to my father; otherwise, as events turned out, I would have known him hardly at all.

The war began in September 1939 and soon we had a soldier staying with us. This procedure of families giving soldiers board and lodging was called billeting, and I can only suppose it saved the government money. I didn't like his uniform which looked scratchy and uncomfortable – khaki-coloured, with canvas gaiters over his big black boots, and a metal helmet shaped

Oakwood Court, from the garden

like a soup plate.

In July 1940, two years after we arrived in Plymouth, and less than a year after war was declared, our twin boy brothers were born, Peter and Paul. Paul died six days later which must have been a tragic event and I know it is one that has troubled Peter throughout his life, yet none of us were told any details about it. What did he die of? Like so much information during that time it was all kept from the children as if they couldn't possibly understand, and it has remained one of the family question marks. The baby who died was originally called Peter, not Paul, but their names were swapped after his death.

Before this birth event we older boys were sent away to stay with Granny and Grandpa Bentall at Oakwood Court; my earliest remembered experience of going away from home and I wasn't happy with it. Our grandparents, while having a lot to offer us, were still very much rooted in a Victorian attitude to children: little boys were to be seen and not heard, allowed to speak only when spoken to and directed by a list of proverbs such as: 'If you don't at first succeed, try, try again,' or if you had a hole in your sock, 'A stitch in time saves nine.' (Socks with holes were darned with wool, not thrown away.) There were no bedtime kisses from Granny and no holding hands. This was a well ordered but austere world, very different from the general friendliness and warmth of home life at that time.

For supper a plate of cornflakes and milk was brought to me in bed in Granny's yellow bathroom.

They must have run out of bedrooms when it came to me as there were often aunts staying. When the dinner gong rang at the foot of the stairs – a hanging copper disc the size of a large plate was banged with a padded stick – for grown-up supper, I was hungry and wanted more than cornflakes so, I raided Granny's biscuit barrel in the adjoining room for extra food. She came up one night convinced that I had been practising dancing in her bedroom. She asked for a demonstration which I was quite unable to give.

But at least my brothers were there. We played a game of makeshift cricket on the lawn with Grandpa bowling and Stuart batting. I was only four so if there were rules, they were a great mystery to me.

My grandfather's fondness for Tudor architecture, even in its artificial form, extended to his house, Oakwood Court, up a lane called Givons Grove between Leatherhead and Dorking in Surrey. It's still very much there, as Hugh, Valeria, Juliet and I looked around it a couple of years ago when it was up for sale - hardly altered in over sixty years since its Bentall days but sadly uncared for. It was probably built in the early nineteen thirties of old red brick and dark oak beams, with a 'minstrels' gallery' over the large drawing room. But instead of real log fires it had false electric ones. Leaded windows showed a garden spreading into the distance and a spoon-shaped gravel driveway swept round to the oak front door. You could hear the scrunching of any approaching car and I always hoped it was someone coming to take me away.

Below a high, walled, paved balcony, on the other

side of the house from the drive, under a big, generous chestnut tree, there was a thirty-foot children's sandpit surrounded by a low picket fence. When you entered through a little wooden gate, in the middle of this sea of sand there was a child-sized house with its own front door and a sign saying 'Woodpecker's Castle.' A smell of damp sand and sticky buds lived around the big tree.

One day Stuart had arranged some of his military Dinky cars in the sand below the parapet. Suddenly they were 'bombed' from above. Grandpa was looking over the balcony wall sending down cushions as missiles,

'Soldiers must expect to be bombed,' he said, like an excited child at playtime.

Some of the toys were broken, so we boys thought the raid too hostile, probably because it was totally unexpected from the acclaimed, but now slightly alien, Chairman and Managing Director. He hadn't built up a habit of playing with us, and children reserve the right to give permission for adults to play with them.

Soon, high in the sky, there were real fights between aircraft. Some would plunge down to earth with black smoke pouring out behind. This was a regular sight in the months ahead. It was the time of 'The Battle of Britain,' when Germany tried to gain supremacy in the air before invading Britain and, fortunately for the world, it didn't quite succeed. Sometimes a German fighter flew low, unexpectedly machine-gunning any civilians in sight. But, loyal to Victorian custom, the real horror of what was going on around us was kept from the children. At six pm, if he was home from the store, Grandpa sat in his comfortable study which contained a large desk, and while smoking a long cigar – probably imagining himself as Winston Churchill – he listened to the BBC news. We were allowed in there, but no-one was allowed to talk. I learnt a lot more about the war from what was called 'the wireless,' than from any of my relatives.

Another ritual was Grandpa's evening walks around his grounds with the two pug dogs: a fat one called Timmy and a slimmer, pleasanter one called Darky. If the pugs dawdled behind on the walk there was a metal bang, bang from the tip of the boss's walking stick on a paving slab, summoning them to catch up as if they were employees instead of dogs. Sometimes we were allowed to go with him while he surveyed his garden and made mental notes about what to tell the gardeners when he next saw them.

Grandpa was so fond of those round, cream-coloured pug dogs that he formed a bad habit after lunch when he was there; he went into a little, sunken scullery room which seemed to have lost its way and hidden itself off the side of the long hallway, and took out a biscuit tin which contained a large sponge cake. He then cut off bits and fed them to the pugs, looking as though he hoped they might perform some tricks in spite of Timmy's obesity. Being wartime, food was strictly rationed to a small quantity for each person. There were no fat people – though, as this was the home of the boss of a big store with a food department, it was not a centre of deprivation – but I was hungry a lot of the time and I felt resentful at seeing those over-fed pugs, looking like rolls of uncooked dough, gobbling up that succulent, syrupy cake. Not one bit of the delicacy came my way as I must have lacked the charm of a pug dog. Timmy, the fat one, bit me one afternoon. He probably felt my cake jealousy and was determined to make sure I was not in the running. He already had to share bits of that massive cake with the slightly trimmer Darky, so all other contenders were to be snapped off in their infancy. I have since tried to make up lost ground by eating sponge cake whenever I see it but those pug dogs are still miles ahead of me.

They had a butler at Oakwood Court in the early days. Grandpa pushed a bell hidden underneath the top of the long dining table and Smith the butler appeared from behind a green baize door nailed with brass studs. Dressed in a black suit he always seemed to be carrying a tray of silver cutlery. Probably he was forever cleaning it so he must have been relieved when the war came so that he could be called up for military service and have a rest from cleaning silver. Stuart told me that this man went on to have a distinguished military career, so others would have been cleaning his brass.

Outside, the flower gardens and herbaceous borders were Granny's great hobby. We boys were often coaxed into picking up flint stones which seemed to multiply ceaselessly in the flower beds. She offered us a halfpenny a barrow load, but this was underpaid hard work, even for a boy situated low to the ground, so no wonder she didn't like doing it herself from a higher altitude. She carried her tools in a flat wooden basket, or trug, and collected little plants wherever she visited, finding a place for them somewhere in one of her borders.

There were three gardeners at Oakwood Court: Bailey, the eldest, was the foreman. Then there was rolly-poly-shaped George, and Jack with a great big forehead where his hair was receding. They all played a prominent part in my childhood because I seemed to spend a lot of time out in the garden. They beamed down an earthy friendliness, in contrast to the stiff, controlled atmosphere of the big house. Although they did all the heavy digging, the gardeners were not allowed to plant anything in Granny's herbaceous borders. Their work was in the vegetable garden, in the rose garden and in the long greenhouses where they grew humid caverns of greeny-smelling tomato plants and cucumbers. These houses were heated by an underground boiler room so that, when the plants were watered, it was, for a small boy, like being in a great rain forest. On the end of these glass buildings was a small, dark potting shed, heavy with the smell of soil and flowerpots. Bamboo canes of all sizes leant in bundles against a corner. On a thick bench opposite the door the gardeners spread out their lunches of enormous cheese and onion sandwiches wrapped in newspaper; at the same time reading the Daily Mirror.

'How long 'r you stayin' this time, Master Christopher?'

'A fortnight I think... How long's a fortnight?'

'Ooh, must be round two weeks or so, maybe.'

A fortnight seemed like a year.

I escaped from a dangerous drowning accident. There was a water-garden with one large, rectangular pond and two smaller ones at the end nearer to the house. On a plinth stood a marble statue of Daphne, running away from Apollo. She was naked except for some bits of laurel sprouting from various parts of her body. You were allowed to see nudes as long as they were the subject of Greek or Roman mythology, nudes for their own sake would have been considered very shocking and 'rude', and not allowed at all. At the statue end of the pond-garden was another huge and mighty chestnut tree. I marvelled at its vast abbey of branches, imagining the difficulties of climbing to the top. If it's still there it must be even bigger, and I wonder if children ever look at it in amazement as I did.

One morning I fell headfirst into one of the small ponds. This was easily done as they were unprotected in any way. Luckily Stuart was nearby and pulled me out as I coughed water bugs and pond weed. Granny was quite calm about it; probably glad she didn't have to report a fatality to my parents. Grandpa reacted with unexpected gentleness, asking if I had seen the fairy who lived at the bottom of the pond. I know I was grateful to Stuart who saved my life by being there, so I was much more pleased to see him than any old fairy.

These long stays with my grandparents, and later with Granny on her own, became ever more frequent and were often without the companionship of my brothers. And because the feelings both of isolation and of a closeness to nature were so strong, the memories of these places are vivid, teaching me to be content in my own company.

THREE

When we returned to our home in Plymouth, following the birth of Peter and Paul, very little was told us about the death of the baby. Possibly, that would have meant talking about birth, and that was definitely not to be mentioned. I was glad to have a younger one in the family smaller than me, even though I would have to wait a while before he was big enough to play with. For his part he must have felt an even greater weight of three brothers above him than I had of two.

We had barely made our acquaintance with each other when a shattering event happened. We had started to become used to the whining rise and fall of the air raid sirens and the deep throbbing fire of the anti-aircraft guns, but one night in December the enemy bombers cut through to Plymouth. They dropped hundreds of fire bombs on the city to destroy the naval harbour, after all, wasn't it the town where Drake had first spotted the Spanish Armada? These bombs were called incendiaries, having the effect of exploding into flames whatever they hit. Our house was in a suburb above the city of Plymouth and was not directly hit but when, in my pyjamas, I looked out of the window with my parents, we saw a widespread land of yellow fire below us. It was strange that my mother and father, instead of being horrified by what they saw, seemed amazingly calm, as if looking at a firework display. Perhaps they felt lucky not to have been blown up but we were looking at hundreds of burning buildings and surely, because it was the late evening, thousands of casualties. It was next morning that we discovered how much damage had been done and how much it was going to affect us.

Father awoke to hear news that his place of work, Dingles Department Store in Plymouth, had been bombed. He no longer had a job. He discussed with Mother the idea of putting up a brass plate outside the front door to advertise himself as an accountant which he may have done for a little while, but it was no good. We had to move.

Father was not passed fit for military service in the war but was soon called to serve in the Admiralty, dealing with Naval operations which, for the time being, solved the job crisis. When he was far from home letters arrived from him with the Admiralty blue oval crest at the top, made more human by his little drawings amongst his sharply angled handwriting. From now on as a family we were to be moved about all over the country, without settling anywhere, until the war ended.

After leaving Plymouth we moved to a temporary home with an elderly vicar and his young wife, the Reverend and Mrs. Green, at Meavy in Devon. He had evidently married a girl who had been in his church choir, which accounted for their wide difference in age. Hugh has told me that her name was Olive Green – surely too good to be true – but she was the first in a long line of my favourite people. In a back pantry of the vicarage she made Devonshire clotted cream by heating milk in a wide, open pan, letting it cool, then skimming the cream off the top. And, as we were in her home at Christmas, she made an important impact on me by giving me my own gramophone record of sung carols. For no obvious reason small and unspectacular actions can leave a deep and lasting impression on us, and I can still hear those special versions of 'Hark the Herald Angels Sing' and 'Oh, Come All Ye Faithful' as if they were the only really worthwhile prototypes – all other versions being pale, unsatisfactory copies. The music seemed to push our troubles briefly into the background. Her personal gift to me had been carefully thought about and in a large family that meant a lot.

Mrs Green had much to endure. Her antique husband always said, every tea time:

'Isn't anyone going to ask me if I'd like another cup of tea?' as if he was totally neglected, which he wasn't.

But his sweet natured wife, though often looking tired and sometimes strained, never complained. She went about her busy life invaded by a family of five – or sometimes six when father visited from his war work – with a continual pleasantness, and she was my first great heroine.

At this point my mother did something which I have always thought heroic. One afternoon Hugh, Stuart and I went for a walk with her along the Devonshire country lanes near the vicarage. Peter had been left in the care of Mrs Green. On our walk the two elder boys took with them a fairly new red metal scooter with white tyres. They started to quarrel:

'It's my turn.'

'No it isn't, you've had a turn!'

Hugh, Stuart, Chris and Peter
on the steps of Meavy Vicarage, 1941

Mother warned them that if they went on arguing she would give the scooter away. Of course they didn't believe her, and the quarrel became worse until they started to shout:

'It's not fair. How can it be fair when you have all the turns!'

At this point a little boy came down the lane towards us.

'Would you like this scooter?' said Mother. 'We'd like to give it to you.'

The boy accepted it with astonishment. My brothers' argument stopped and they stared in silence as their precious scooter was scooted away by a complete stranger, never to be seen again. I wonder how that boy was received by his parents, arriving home with precious and unexpected, dream wheels. The complete truth he told must have been hard to believe.

Then came a horrible experience for me which had such a bad effect that it has taken me a lifetime to come to terms with it. Without any warning or explanation my mother suddenly announced that I was to be sent away again to stay with Granny Bentall. This time it was to be on my own without any of my brothers and without any idea of when I was coming back. Stuart had already been sent away to boarding school in Surrey, and Hugh to one in Cornwall, while Peter, barely one year old, was naturally to stay with Mother. She had made the important decision to relinquish her three elder sons for most of the year, and I believe she never ever truly got them back.

It must have been autumn or winter. I recall the bleakness of the landscape when Miss Ford, the silent and icy governess employed by my grandmother, arrived at Meavy to take me away. On the long train journey Miss Ford said nothing to me while my heart gradually cracked into pieces. It was a single railway carriage separated from others by a narrow corridor outside a sliding door. I watched the endless brown fields and forked winter trees slide past, giving me absolutely no understanding why I was being taken away from home at the age of five. Feeling as if I had crossed the world to end up in prison, on arrival at Oakwood Court I cried continually for three days. I couldn't believe what seemed to be the treachery of my mother who had explained nothing and had not acknowledged my distress before I left. I screamed inside at the joyless, comfortable protocol of my grandmother's home. Granny Bentall was moved by my tears and, desperate for a remedy, bribed me to stop crying by giving me an old wrist watch, which still worked, that she found in a drawer.

Not thriving, a doctor was called to examine me. This time instead of the usual Scottish lady Doctor Blair, who visited us when needed during our stays with Granny, this time it was a Specialist, probably brought from London, dressed in a black suit with big white cuffs. I was very similar to the dormouse in A. A. Milne's poem, 'The Dormouse and the Doctor,' who just wanted delphiniums (blue) and geraniums (red) instead of what was thought best for him; similarly there was no cure for me from a doctor. The consultant tapped my chest and my back and listened through his stethoscope, but had no medicine for acute homesickness, which to me felt like a terminal illness.

Grandpa must have been around at the time but I don't remember his being involved in any part of this, though he may have given his permission for the expensive Specialist.

The noises of war thundered on in this area of Surrey with gunfire, and aeroplanes fighting in the sky. Long, long lines of army lorries amassed in the road below Oakwood Court, many of them with the red maple leaf of Canada painted on the front. I saw The Royal Canadian Engineers build the new road leading off to Bookham at this time, later called Young Street, after Colonel Young who was the commander in charge.

Again I took up my friendship with the gardeners, watching their methodical digging of a flower bed, like a rising tide gradually cutting into a beach. Then another favourite person began to cast her influence on my life. This was Aunty Joy, my mother's sister, older than her by one year. She lived in a happy house in Oxshott, not far from Leatherhead. It had lattice windows and a big open hallway with everything leading off it, like a railway booking hall from where you went on different journeys through the house.

Auntie Joy had little of her own hair. It never grew properly, so she wore a wig. But she was so kind and had so much time for children, especially for me, that, like all imperfections of those we are fond of, her shortages of hair became forgotten. I stayed with her from time to time and there were woods opposite her house, with a pond where, with a small net, I could go fishing for tadpoles and sticklebacks. She allowed me to store my catches in jam jars in her garage, while I watched for frogs. She had a long-haired Dachshund called Wizard who was endlessly agreeable, making up for the scarcity of her owners' hair as Aunty Joy's husband, Cecil Elliott, also lacked hair. He was an Air Force pilot, doing air-sea rescue work. He must have been in some hostile action because he had a piece of one ear missing. He was also a keen golf enthusiast and while I was still young I sometimes acted as his caddy, carrying around a heavy bag containing clubs with highly imaginative and eccentric names like 'Mashie Niblick.' He showed me how to hold a putter with the little finger of the bottom hand locked around the forefinger of the top one – rather like, I imagine, a Freemason's handshake. My reward for this dedication to his golf was a ginger ale outside the clubhouse as I was too young to be allowed into its revered interior.

Cecil and Joy had a sunken bath in their bathroom which was very unusual, and an exciting experience for a child. You looked out over the rim at floor level, too low for the easy reach of grown-ups. There was a printed poem of instructions by the bath, asking you to keep the room tidy, illustrated with encouraging pictures of pink, pudgy, smiling toddlers by Mabel Lucie Attwell. The poem began:

'Please remember, don't forget,

Never leave the bathroom wet...'

One night, when they thought I was asleep, I heard them saying kind things about me. There are few things more helpful to a child's self-esteem than that.

Whereas at Oakwood Court we never saw the mechanics of the kitchen because it was all run by staff behind closed doors, and if I had been discovered there it would have been considered trespassing, at Aunty Joy's everything was there to be enjoyed: toasters popped up, grills sizzled, pastry was rolled and jam was spooned into tarts. She encouraged me to make pastry mice with string tails and current eyes. She mowed the lawn and I collected up the long grass with a wire rake and, though I suffered runny eyes from the dry grass, it was a good way of making hay for somebody's rabbit.

She had a cupboard in her living room full of games to play, like Ludo, Peggity and packs of opened and unopened playing cards. There was also a large and colourful collection of cigarette cards with different picture subjects, each block held together with elastic bands. Sets of fish, birds, animals and sportsmen had all been collected by a devoted smoker, or a team of smokers as there would be one card in each packet of cigarettes. The house appeared full of light without any oppressive corners. By the fireplace was a metal effigy of a knight in pewter-coloured armour holding the hearth brush and the fire poker with obedient good humour. Aunty Joy's house was always a welcome, light-hearted contrast to the large, brown, cavernous cathedral of Oakwood Court.

Later on this favourite Aunt was to pass the greatest test a child can set an adult; she kept an important promise. It was when I was about seven and going to Downsend School each day from Granny's, taking the number 470 bus from the bottom of Givons Grove to Leatherhead. I was desperately keen at the time to own a fishing rod so that I could accompany an older boy called Alan Willoughby on his trips to the river. Aunty Joy said she would buy me a rod, and as I walked up Givons Grove after school I knew she was going to be at the house, but kept saying to myself,

'She won't have bought it. Grown ups don't do that sort of thing in real life. They just promise things, but she won't have bought it.'

I went in to The Loggia, a room used a lot in that house (now it might be called a conservatory). Aunty Joy was sitting down and pointed calmly to a corner of the room. There, in a brown, fabric case was a gloriously glossy wooden fishing rod, complete with reel. Angelic are those adults who keep their promises to children. An insignificant, unremembered action by someone in a brief moment of their life can sometimes have such a powerful effect on a child that its life may be transformed for ever. The fishing rod gave me many hours of pleasure even though I never caught anything; perhaps teaching me that neither by skill nor inclination am I a natural hunter. I'll gather while others hunt.

Sadly, Joy developed muscular sclerosis and declined in health, gradually drifting away from me when I was a teenager. I don't believe she had any idea how valuable she was to me or how much affection and respect I had for her but, although she had no children of her own and would have been a marvellous mother, her maternal gifts were given to me just at a time when they had their maximum benefit. She didn't have to be a mother to mother brilliantly.

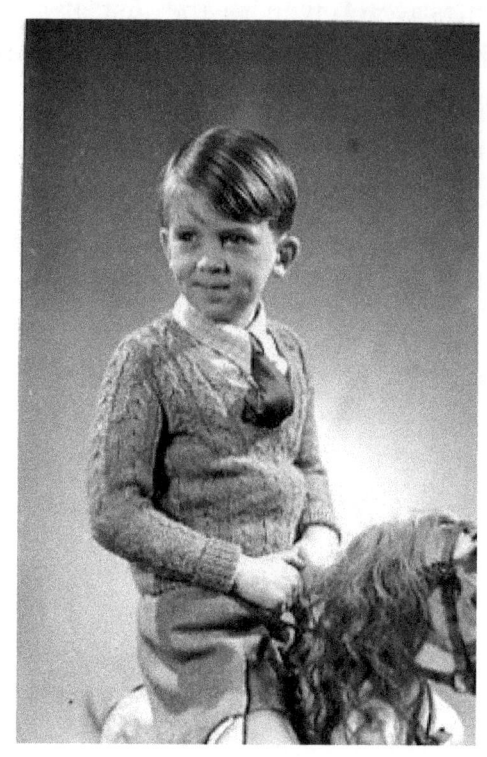

Chris modelling a jumper
for a women's magazine, 1943

FOUR

Evidently life had become too difficult at Meavy vicarage in spite of the reduced number of lodgers, so, as our family needed to be together briefly for a school holiday, we moved into Smith, the butler's, flat over the garage at Oakwood Court, empty because he had left his household duties and the shiny cutlery to start an illustrious career in the army.

This was a chaotic time of comings and goings and, like most of my childhood, it is impossible for me or anyone else to remember what happened when. Like all families without their own homes, our welcome wore thin wherever we went and those who took us in, though seeing our homeless situation, soon, I'm sure, found it too much of a strain. Four boys during school holidays, a mother and an occasionally visiting father were a lot of people to accommodate.

A time of respite and what seemed like a little bit of security followed. We rented a flat in Wimbledon – not the safest of places, being on a flight path between Germany and London – but the Grainger Grandparents lived just round the corner with Father's sister, Muriel. She helped me with my reading and we became close friends later in life when she lived to an old age. One day during the Wimbledon time she invited me to pose for a photograph in a London studio, modelling a knitting pattern for a jumper. Muriel was the editor of a weekly women's magazine which had need of such things and I sat for the picture on a rocking horse, but not without nervous tears. My

Tim Plowright in Dykelands garden, June 1953

self confidence was low; I never knew when the next departure would come or when my trunk would be packed and put with me onto a train.

At this point I had a handsome blue tricycle all of my own, which puzzles me now I think about it because every bit of metal was being used to make guns and bombs, even railings and gates were being cut down and taken away to the munitions factories. Yet here I was, pedalling around Raymond Court on a three-wheeler which seemed brand new to me. Things arrived, or were taken away, without explanation.

Now a new figure entered our lives and was going to lodge himself into our future more and more permanently. He had been mentioned by Mother as a genial friend who loved children, called Uncle Tim. He, Tim Plowright, was the instrument which was to destroy our parents' marriage. He was to become our stepfather and in doing so to overwhelm both us, as a family of boys, and himself. Exempt from war service because he was a pharmacist, one night he arrived at the flat in an atmosphere full of shadows. Instead of the smiling figure we had been led to expect he barely acknowledged Peter and me. Hugh and Stuart were away at school. Tim, with his black hair and moustache, seemed to slide in sideways through the door and sometime during the night he must have slid out again.

He had known Lilian a long time, even before her marriage to Geoffrey and it is probably true to say that they were more naturally suited to each other than she was to our father. They liked the formality of dressing up and going to dinners and conferences connected with the Pharmaceutical Society where he worked. Mother was an excellent cook so she enjoyed entertaining in the rather formal way that pleased Tim. She was also an enthusiastic and clever needlewoman. Neither of them was interested in reading, music or theatre but they found a circle of friends connected with pharmacy. Tim was tidy and meticulous. Grapes were to be cut from the bunch with special silver scissors, never picked off. Car doors were to be closed quietly, never slammed, and neckties were to be sober in design, even those of young men, and chosen according to such old-fashioned rules as: 'Blue and green should never be seen,' and 'Colours should never clash.' To me and my brothers, being at a critical age, he and his friends seemed pompous and unimaginative.

By contrast, Father loved music, was a good 'cellist, and his idea of dressing up was to appear in amateur theatrical productions, which often embarrassed Lilian. He read widely, introducing me to Greek and Roman myths and to A. A. Milne's poems. With excitement he took us to pantomimes and ice shows. He lacked outward style or the ability to make difficult things look easy, and could become flustered under pressure. He never mastered the ability to deal with waiters or waitresses who always seemed to serve his table last and bring the wrong dish, no matter how polite he was. He had a satirical sense of humour, was highly intelligent yet retained a childlike quality. He was not at all practical but had highly practical sons. When he came back into my life very many years later, he 'phoned me one morning in a panic saying that he had borrowed someone's 'cello and somehow made a hole in the top of it. Could I mend it? So I did my very best with a small insert of suitable wood, staining it and lightly varnishing it. It wasn't perfect and I wondered how he could have possibly have created a hole in the top of a 'cello. Evidently the good lady owner didn't seem worried about it and accepted the repair without comment. Perhaps it was her fourth or fifth very best 'cello, thank goodness. Father was good at making up indoor games, writing playlets and sketches, and putting words into the mouths of stuffed toys, or real animals if any happened to be around. He could be sharply critical and Conservative in outlook but he won many friends with his humour and lack of pomposity.

So Father and Tim Plowright could hardly have been more different and Mother probably chose the wrong husband in the first place. She told us that, before the marriage, when her parents considered her too young to become involved with Geoffrey, she was sent away to a 'finishing school' in Switzerland where young ladies learnt how to run houses but not how to be mothers. Father wrote letters to her during this time of separation; these must have been so charming, skilled and entertaining that when she returned from the snowy Alps she was even more determined to marry him.

Tim remained a shadowy figure for many years, slipping in and out of our homes like a villain in a silent film, all the while thinking himself the romantic hero until he achieved what he wanted and married

Lilian in 1952 while we were all away at school. At this time she made her greatest error. She issued an order to her sons forbidding that Father's name should ever be mentioned. He was now to be known as C.S. – Closed Subject. No contact with him was allowed. Granny Bentall tried to bring us together, and tried to make it possible for us to accept his presents but Mother's stubbornness, encouraged by Tim, prevailed.

Many years passed with this unhappy situation and only after we were all married did we, one by one, see Father again. Divisions had arisen in the family between those who were unquestioningly loyal to Mother and those who felt a natural kinship to Father. By this time Tim had died of Leukaemia early in 1960 but Mother never, right to the end of her life in 1990, admitted our right to see our father which had caused a fifteen year split between her and me.

In December 1942, aged six, I was off again to Granny's from Wimbledon because I remember being in the garden at Oakwood Court, watching my grandfather showing a group of sea cadets how to saw through the trunk of a large tree which had been felled earlier. They were using a cross-saw with one person at each end gripping a handle. This is a sight not seen now that there are chain-saws, but then it was the common way of cutting through thick timber. Grandpa must have put too much energy and enthusiasm into the demonstration, being more accustomed to mental rather than physical work, for he died of a heart attack that night aged sixty seven. He never experienced retirement, and left Bentalls of Kingston without its Chairman and Managing Director but in a position to continue from strength to strength.

I went to his memorial service in Kingston church where a young chorister sang 'Oh, For the Wings of a Dove', and all the grown ups around me in their dark clothes seemed particularly tall and thin, as if I was standing in a plantation of black bamboos.

Life at Oakwood Court was to change very gradually. Granny grew warmer and was to expand as a caring influence in her grandsons' lives. She stayed on in the big house until 1947, with much the same routine as before. Many elderly ladies visited for tea. One of the regulars was a small, bird-like lady called Miss Tight. I knew nothing about her. She alighted frequently then flew off. Brown bread and honey, cress sandwiches and fruit cake were all administered by Granny from a tea-trolley; sponge cake still being reserved for the pugs.

My grandmother introduced me to the family who had just moved into the white Regency style manor house across the fields, where I made friends with a little girl called Venetia Stopford-Adams. She had a younger sister called Charmian and we played on their beautiful grey rocking horse. Aged seven I learnt my first lesson in tactics with girls. One afternoon I arrived there to find Venetia's mood very aloof. After a little while some instinct stirred:

'Oh well, I took the trouble to come and play with you. If you aren't interested I'll just go away again.

The Grainger Band, 1953

That's fine by me.'

I started to walk away then she spoke,

'No, please stay. I wanted you to come.'

She was testing out her feminine power. After that we were excellent friends. Unfortunately I wasn't always able to use this cool wisdom later on when I fell in love. Expectation can cause disappointment.

I was nearly burnt in a flaming heap when I set a haystack on fire in Oakwood Court garden. The hay was used to feed some cattle in the field which lay between Granny's and where Venetia lived and I climbed onto the top of the haystack to see into the distance without anyone seeing me. One hot afternoon I was experimenting with a magnifying glass or with some matches and a cigarette, I really don't remember, when suddenly the whole thing caught fire and I had to jump for my life.

Granny kept remarkably cool considering she lost all her winter hay. She thought of some suitable punishment, like writing out a hundred times:

'I must not set fire to haystacks.'

Then the episode was forgotten by her, but not by a thin, elderly aunt called Hazel who had moved in as Granny's companion. After the haystack incident she always viewed me with deep suspicion. To her I was a delinquent, right up to the time she died many years later. It amused me that whenever I came anywhere near Hazel she became nervous, as if thinking:

'Put away the matches; hide your handbag; Christopher's here.'

'Maiden Aunts' or 'Spinsters' are not known

nowadays but were plentiful in the 1940s because they were the female generation who had lost potential boyfriends and husbands in the First World War, which had ended in 1918. Without marriages, children or careers, many grew prematurely old, cold and critical and, though deserving compassion, they seldom seemed to form firm attachments to children.

After five years of running Oakwood Court without Grandpa, in 1947, after the war ended, Granny moved to Hunterscombe, a large bungalow situated the other side of a high wire fence at the far end of Oakwood Court grounds. The big house was then taken over by Gerald Bentall, Mother's eldest brother, who had become Chairman and Managing Director of the successful store. His most stylish and energetic second wife, Joy, immediately set about changing all the dark oak furniture of Oakwood Court into light-grey, limed oak. She seemed to have connections with the London art world and became a governor of The Royal College of Art. She seemed altogether too high-powered to be of any artistic help to me, like a speedboat rushing past a cork.

They gave, for a number of years, big Christmas parties at Oakwood Court. Gerald, dressed up as Father Christmas, was seen to approach the house over a wintry garden and then hand out presents to the large gathering of his own and his wife's family. Usually a shy and withdrawn man, Gerald, when hidden inside his red, fur-lined costume of largesse, seemed to enjoy playing the part. Later he was to do a great deal more for us brothers than dip into a sack.

These big family parties were an important motivation for our Grainger Brothers' Band to develop and perform. Hugh was always a fine organiser and ran the show from his drum kit at the back. Stuart, a highly gifted musician, played the piano accordion with great gusto even though he had very few lessons. I started by playing ukulele-banjo until, aged fourteen, my brothers convinced me that clarinet was just the right instrument for me to learn, even though I had absolutely no idea what a clarinet was or what it looked like. I became very glad they made this choice for me because my ability to play traditional jazz later on as a young man gave me a lot of pleasure and social acceptance. Peter took over as the banjo player in our family line-up and we trotted our way through medleys of old-favourite tunes, specialising in a list of nice waltzes. We sat behind homemade varnished music stands with 'GB' – Grainger Band – painted on the front. As none of us could actually read music there was not much for the music stands to do except carry lists of what came next.

At one Oakwood Court Christmas we did a lively performance of the poem, 'The Pied Piper of Hamlyn,' reciting the words between us and playing our own music and effects, such as the clarinet doing trills to represent the rats, and drums the vanished children.

All this creativity helped to form us into an increasingly self-supporting unit. It made us feel more secure and comfortable but also tended to cut us off from other youngsters of our own ages as we looked within the family for friendship. All of us, I think, found girls a distant and fascinating mystery for a longer time than most boys. We just didn't know how to approach them.

Before the final party at Oakwood Court, after which they were held for a couple of years at Gerald and Joy's new, custom built house at Witley, Surrey, Hugh organised the making of a toy garage to be given as a present to their young son, David. On the back of the wooden building was screwed a small metal plate, engraved by me, which said:

'Made by Grainger Brothers, England.'

FIVE

As early as the time we were living at Meavy vicarage, when I was five, I had been sent to a local village infant school. It had not been a pleasant experience; an abrasive teacher and an unattractive school room had not appealed to me in any way. Then when we went to Wimbledon I was sent to The Squirrel School which seemed to have only one teacher; a woman who, to my young eyes, seemed to have been dipped in oil. Often she nodded off into a snooze. The grey uniform and cap we had to wear matched the greasy greyness of the teacher and it is difficult to imagine how anyone could teach so little, or that a school could be so pointless.

The daily walks to school were across Wimbledon Common. On the grass were lines of anti-aircraft guns, their barrels angled towards the sky. They blasted out a huge noise whenever an enemy plane came near, by day or night. In the sky were fat barrage balloons floating like silver elephants on the end of ropes to discourage low-flying German aircraft. When I hear loud fireworks today it brings back the tearing gunfire angrily trying to hack enemy aircraft out of the sky. On Wimbledon common was a pond where I sailed paper boats.

There was little colour among the people of that world. The population seemed to camouflage itself in drab clothes and hats. There were no street or shop lights, and windows were covered with black fabric at night so that enemy aeroplanes had no targets to fix upon. Dark cream was the universal colour of interior walls once the Edwardian wallpaper had worn out or fallen off.

I was sent to stay with Granny Bentall again and went daily to Downsend School in Leatherhead by taking the bus each way from Oakwood Court. Although the inside of the school smelt distantly of Jeyes Fluid disinfectant, I recognised that it was a good private school, in a Victorian building with its own playing fields, just outside Leatherhead town. The fact that the school was perfectly situated to attract whatever bombs German air-crews felt like dropping near London made the job of the Headmaster, Mr Linford, and teachers very difficult.

We had many air-raids. These were signalled by a loud siren wailing with sliding-up-and-down notes when an attack was just about to arrive, warning everyone to take cover. When the raid was over, a long sustained note told people that they could emerge from their shelters or cellars or any other hiding place. You could not ignore these siren warnings; they were powerful and threatening. Often in the middle of school lunches the moaning sound started and we scuttled under the tables for supposed protection like burrowing animals; the idea being that if the ceiling fell down the tables would stop our being totally crushed. As things became more and more dangerous we went deeper, ever more hunted, and spent air raids in the underground boiler room, which felt much safer than a dining room table over our heads as bombs exploded nearby. Soon we were to spend whole nights down there, sleeping on mattresses on the floor.

I was now blessed with another marvellous woman in my life; this was my young form mistress, Mary Lee. She was a caring, gifted teacher, keen on crafts as well as reading, writing and sums. She even encouraged us to paint. We made cross-stitch belts for our mothers, showing us the basics of sewing with big needles and coloured wool, and we painted portraits of our parents from memory. Mine seemed so far away. I desperately wanted to make a good likeness but didn't have the skill. Miss Lee took a real interest in each one of us. To us she was beautiful and we loved her.

In spite of the hardships that all schools must have been going through, there were astonishingly beautiful moments. This school staged a brilliant production of 'A Christmas Carol' by Charles Dickens. A very convincing set was revealed when the stage curtains opened, unlike much open-stage theatre today, and at the end of the play snow, just like the real thing, dropped from above, covering the stage with white magic.

For some strange reason this particular school routine was broken again for me when I was sent for a short time back to the Squirrel School in Wimbledon, just as unsuccessfully as before. Perhaps my mother was feeling little pangs of guilt, forgetting what I looked like. It certainly wasn't for my safety, as Wimbledon was just as likely to be bombed as Leatherhead. But this odd diversion didn't last long and I was returned to Downsend as a boarder. My preparations for boarding school were supervised, not by mother, but by my grandmother, who fitted me out with the correct clothes and packed my trunk. Looking back I wonder how decisions about us as children were made. I felt like a small hoop being thrown over a series of posts, forgotten until someone decided to throw me onto the next. But I could never work out who was doing the throwing. No-one owned up. No-one discussed it or explained.

Luckily when I returned to Downsend I was again in Mary Lee's class. All of us, staff and boys now felt a real sense of danger. We were given a warning lecture by a man from the War Office, telling us not to touch any found object which might look interesting, as German aircraft were dropping things designed to fascinate children – called anti-personnel bombs – which might be of any tempting shape, looking like a fountain pen perhaps or a toy, and vary in size. If you picked one up it would explode and probably kill you. These were designed to demoralise the civilian population and cause a general lack of hope, but in my memory everyone seemed to become more and more determined. Also at this time, all over the local landscape, there were lengths of paper tape – about an inch wide, silver on one side and matt black on the other. Evidently, Stuart told me, these were dropped by British aeroplanes to confuse the German radar system. Schoolboys collected a lot of this stuff as it wasn't dangerous to pick up, but soon we really didn't know what to use it for, so it stayed on the ground.

Then the 'flying bombs' or 'Doodlebugs' arrived. These were pilotless aircraft packed with explosives. After the siren warned us of approaching danger we heard the very distinctive raw engine noise, like a tractor, overhead. Then it suddenly stopped. We waited in total silence to hear where and on whom the killing contraption would drop. After one raid we came out of our shelter and discovered that a bomb had exploded on the playing field, making a huge hole near the school buildings. Although there was some excitement to see the physical evidence of the explosion, even we immature children quickly realised that this crater, a couple of hundred yards nearer, could have easily blown us to pieces.

Then, early in 1944, news came that a bomb had struck our Wimbledon home. Peter and Mother were out of the flat that night staying with a Swiss woman friend down the road. If they had been at home the bomb could have injured or killed them as it had gone straight through the bedroom ceiling. Like me, Hugh and Stuart were away at different schools. Once more we were a homeless family.

Quickly the decision was made that it was too dangerous for children to stay around London any longer and a mass evacuation began. Mary Lee, our school saviour, offered to take the boarders in her class away to her parents' cottage near Stoke-on-Trent for the remaining ten weeks of the summer term. Six of us travelled there by train and slept in the cottage, two to a bed. There was an outside earth closet lavatory at the end of the garden with two wooden seats side by side – a co-habitable loo? – and plenty of those spiders which love unheated outside buildings. We loved being with Miss Lee. Her aproned mother prepared meals while we went through a pretence of lessons. The upheaval and lack of school books must have made her teaching very difficult, but her kindness and grace was more important to us than lessons. In the afternoons we walked across damp fields of long grass wearing Wellington boots, for the early summer must have been wet. We even played a simple game of cricket with Mary Lee in those cow pastures, and splashed our way through shallow streams at the side of the road. She allowed us to draw pictures of guns and submarines, of battles and Spitfire aeroplanes because, though she too was young, she understood that children in war need to express what they know of the unknown to help them accept the chaos, and in some tiny, ineffectual way to feel they are contributing something to a situation they are powerless to change.

When eventually the summer term ended and we were returned by train to our mothers, I had to say goodbye forever to dear Mary Lee, my first love. I hope she found a very caring husband and had her own children who would have enjoyed the most perfect mother. This would have been her proper reward. How I would like to tell all those magnificent people how priceless their gifts to us were. We were much too young at the time to show them proper appreciation.

It was to be a good summer holiday. After the bombing of the Wimbledon flat we were again on offer to the kindness of relatives. I met up with my mother and brothers to stay at the house of Uncle Mortimer – Granny's brother – and his wife Decima, at Bewdley, Worcestershire. They hardly knew us at all. There were two rather superior teenage daughters, Rosemary and Janet, and although Rosemary was less often there, being a student nurse, there was only just enough room for us all to stay for the eight weeks of the school holiday. Father had become an even more distant figure now, visiting seldom.

Janet, the younger daughter, had a little green shed in the garden where she did carpentry. My elder brothers remember her as being very accommodating to them, allowing them to try sawing wood, or bang in nails. But it was different for me. Eight-year-old boys to teenage girls are a total waste of space and my puny efforts at carpentry were ridiculed. I was banished from the shed. Not to worry. I had a very colourful cardboard cut-out book of a country cottage with its garden and detailed flower beds. It had tiny seats and green lawns where I could escape in my imagination. Decima helped me cut out the bits and glue them together; she was a kindly, grey haired woman who died in 1997 aged ninety seven.

There were thick woods near the house and because it was summer the ferns grew high, green and dense. Peter was old enough now, at four, to join in our games, so, under Hugh's direction, we formed a military style squad, disappearing into the forest of ferns which grew well above our heads. The older boys made badges for us to wear and we took on all the enemies of the world in imaginary combat.

I returned to Granny's for a while. She was a committed member of the Congregational Church in

Granny Bentall, c. 1950

Leatherhead. Whichever one of us was staying went with her to that church on Sundays and filed out to children's classes just before the sermon. The whole place was rather too scrubbed-looking for me, like the day room of a well-ordered clinic. The choir ladies wore blue gowns and flat blue hats like squashed boxes on their heads. Even as a child I preferred churches with candles and an air of mystery, though where I had experienced such churches is a mystery; perhaps earlier at Meavy with Mrs Green and her vicar husband.

Granny's church only became interesting when I became a teenager. Stuart and I once went to a party held in the church hall where there was dancing and I made a miniscule friendship with an attractive girl whose face I remember to this day. Although I didn't find the scrubbed church agreeable, scrubbed girls I liked, with a little touch of lipstick they had found from somewhere.

My grandmother's great strength was not in taking us to church, or her long list of proverbs: 'A bird in the hand is worth two in the bush;' 'Waste not, want not;' 'A thing worth doing is worth doing well,' but her extraordinary ability to tune into each person's need as an individual. This gift became stronger as we grew older. For example, when her house sign 'Hunterscombe' needed re-painting she entrusted me with the job, even though I had very little experience of painting signs. To be trusted by her in spite of everything was a great builder of my confidence, so that sign writing became an occasional, profitable sideline. If there were important notices to be displayed in her

The Shakespeare Hotel, Stratford on Avon, 1949

church she asked me to write them in special lettering, giving me the foundations to see myself as a craftsman, and how we see ourselves is vitally important.

Somehow detecting my interest in picture-making – she must have been very observant to see it, as I wasn't a child who was always drawing – she somehow arranged a visit to an eminent artist's studio. Yes, I think the studios of the 19th Century really were how we imagine them; it was a very Victorian interior with brown drapes and masses of large furniture, as if banishing the light rather than welcoming it. Granny and I sat on a *chaise longue* while we talked with the artist about the different characteristics of oil paint and watercolour.

'Watercolour is a long apprenticeship,' said the artist.

This remark made me fearful of using watercolour for a very long time. If the great artist found it challenging, who was I to try it? His attitude still persists. People either think of watercolours – as Dylan Thomas put it in his play, 'Under Milk Wood' – "like lettuce salad dying." Or people say it's too difficult because you can't change it. But when I discovered its brilliance by using tubes of watercolour rather than those little pans you find in watercolour boxes, and keeping the colours separate by mixing them on different white plates, then I found it suited me very well. And if you use top quality watercolour paper you can wash most of an unwanted colour away with clean water, a paintbrush and absorbent cloth.

Granny took me to a performance of Elgar's 'The

Dream of Gerontius' which didn't light me up at the time, but she was about to do something magnificent which really did change my life for the better. It was an enormously powerful event which has affected me always: On August 31 1949 she arranged for me to go, with a couple of young married cousins of hers, Gordon and Mary, to Stratford-on-Avon for two days.

We stayed at the Shakespeare Hotel with its leaded windows and oak beams. Here every room was named after a character in a Shakespeare play. This appealed to me even though I knew nothing about the theatre. I didn't know anything about staying in hotels either; the next morning I was confused about whether I should make my bed before going down to breakfast. We went to a performance of 'A Midsummer Night's Dream' which was not only astonishing in its beauty but extremely funny. It was thoughtful to take me to a play which made me laugh as an introduction to Shakespeare; anything else might have put me off, but this experience attracted me so much to the theatre, to Shakespeare and to Stratford-on-Avon that I still find it a thrilling experience just to be there. With my young married companions we bought souvenirs and went to Anne Hathaway's cottage. There was no doubt they were just as excited by the trip as I was.

It is still a mystery how Granny spotted these interests in me and I am very appreciative of the different ways she thought up to help them along. She was never demonstrative but became easier to talk to as we grew older. Silently she seemed to ask herself:

'Now what can I do for him I wonder. What are

his interests?'

And then she came up with an answer which would lead to action.

She was always frugal and the family used to say that she would have been a good wife to a poor man. A knotted piece of string was never thrown away but had to be untied and used again. I never knew you could buy wrapping paper because Granny always re-used old bits; socks and woollens were constantly darned and clothes were knitted. When I stayed with her I often had to hold out my hands, like an angler describing a fish, with a skein of wool stretched between them so that she could then wind the wool into a large ball.

But when she gave presents, only the best quality would do. I had a fine pigskin travelling bag from her with my initials on the side – a good gift for a boy who was always travelling, and I still have my blue, leather-bound Bible with my name on the front in gold leaf. When I was five, when we were at Meavy, she gave me a great present, 'The Children's Art Book.' It had a variety of art pictures – Hokusai's 'Wave' for example in colour, though mostly the pictures were in black and white, it being wartime, by both prominent and less well-known artists. On each page it chatted about the pictures in a friendly way so that a child was drawn into the whole process of picture-making. Did she give me the book because she had picked up that I would be interested in art? Or did I become interested in art as a result of receiving the book?

She was happiest gardening and feeding the chickens, ducks and guinea fowl which thrived in large runs at the bottom of Oakwood Court, then Hunterscombe garden. Jack Busk, the middle gardener from earlier days had come to be her helper. He did the heavy gardening, dealt with the poultry, including plucking feathers and cleaning them out ready for cooking – which made me want to be a lifelong vegetarian though I didn't become one – and he was her chauffeur too, able to convert quickly from garden dungarees to dark suit and cap at a moment's notice, driving the maroon Austin wherever she wanted to go. Usually when we came to stay in her Hunterscombe days we arrived by train at Dorking Deepdene Station, which still looks much the same today in 2013 as it did then. Granny was always there when we arrived, standing with her brown, floral umbrella, ready to greet us in her quiet way. But whenever possible we would take the bus. She somehow arranged for the local council to place a bus stop near her front gate. Jack Busk was totally loyal. We knew him over many years. On Granny's death he went to work on Gerald Bentall's newly acquired estate in Witley, Surrey, living in a little cottage in the grounds with a lately-married wife.

My last view of Granny Bentall was on Brighton railway station in 1954. I was going away from home again; this time to Aldershot, aged eighteen, to join up for my National Service in the army. She, not my mother, came to say goodbye at the station. She died in her sleep of a heart attack a few weeks later. She had been the essential pivotal character during a very unstable period and although I had not appreciated her as a four year old, I had come to value her as the magnificent guiding influence in my early life; for the way she had taken a continual interest in my interests. She had shown her great love in actions, not words.

With Peter; St. Christopher's school, 1946

SIX

At the end of 1944 Mother decided to rent a maisonette, in the middle of the town of Hove, just over the border from Brighton. Maisonette is a strange word meaning little house, but this wasn't particularly small. It was a cream-painted Regency building with lots of rooms coming off the staircase at different levels and a woman living in the basement. To help pay the rent to start with we had a Canadian ice hockey player staying in one room. At Brighton ice rink they had professional matches so I suppose he must have played for Brighton. He was strong and handsome but seemed a little depressed, probably because his wife and family were apart from him in Canada.

Life began to gather a little more security again after my evacuation to Stoke-on-Trent and the stay at Bewdley. Mother had certainly chosen Hove as a place to settle because it was Tim Plowright's home town. This made our father Geoffrey's efforts to re-establish himself back with his family after the war impossible. It was his own family but he was not welcomed by his wife so, unfortunately, he became short-tempered with his boys as if they were accomplices in the betrayal, which of course they weren't. Tim, Tim's elderly father, his married sister, Norah and her husband, Hardie Williamson, were introduced increasingly into our lives and it was just a question of time before the marriage collapsed and our father went away for ever in 1948.

Norah and Hardie were artists and keen gardeners,

Hugh, Stuart, Chris and Peter
on the West Pier, Brighton, 1948

living not far away in Henfield. He was a commercial glass designer and taught at The Royal College of Art, but even they didn't escape Tim Plowright's imperious attitude to all things artistic. He used to refer to them, and to me, as 'Arty Crafty.' His attitudes were born of a limited knowledge of the world. Having escaped war service he had travelled hardly at all. The world seems more threatening to those with little experience of it. Also, men who didn't serve in the war were nervous of criticism from those who did, so they often stuck together with others who had remained civilians, to avoid arguments which, for a time, did break out.

I liked the house in Lansdown Place, Hove, very much because it was near a great variety of shops and near the seafront, with the West and Palace Piers and all their vulgar, seductive attractions. Bumper cars, boating pools – 'Come in, Number Seven, your time's up!' – and slot machines soon returned after the war, though, when we first arrived, the beaches still contained land mines, with notices warning the public to stay away, and very heavy concrete blocks like experimental pyramids and cubes stood all along the edge of the sea to frustrate a German invasion. I was sent to a day school in Hove called St. Christopher's, with a bright red cap and blazer. I remember very little about the school except some hymns in the morning and the headmaster, Mr Beale, trying to teach us French pronunciation:

'You say "Eh," but your mouth should be in the shape of "Ooh," he instructed.

Our French didn't progress much further than this,

Aldro from the front drive, 1946

but there were teachers who managed to teach less.

Nothing else captured my imagination. I felt mentally exhausted with all the changes of homes and schools. This was my sixth school entry in four years, and a rebellious spirit stirred within me. Sometimes I played truant and spent the day on the pier, slipping what pennies I had into slot machines. It is surprising the school never contacted my mother to find out where I was. I could have been anywhere.

The war with Germany – but not yet with Japan – ended on May 7th 1945 and to celebrate there was a big firework display on Hove sea-front. I went with Mother and Father. There were not many bangers, people were tired of explosions, but there were huge portraits, picked out in contours of white fire, of King George VI and Queen Elizabeth (who later became The Queen Mother) who had faithfully supported the British population throughout the war, putting themselves in danger in London instead of running away to some place of safety. I wondered what the creative people who had made this grand display had been doing in the war, and where all these fireworks had come from so suddenly. Had a group of keen, secret enthusiasts, in some ammunitions factory somewhere, put aside a pile of gunpowder every so often and turned out an odd box of fireworks when no-one was looking, pretending it was a special bomb they were fussing over? Well, however these things were made, we were glad of them now.

Until 1946 Hugh and Stuart had been going to

Aldro from the lake, 1946

separate preparatory schools: Hugh, to Kings School, Canterbury Junior School which was evacuated during the war to Carlyon Bay in Cornwall. This made sense when we were all living in Devon, but he became increasingly separated as our fortunes took us around the south of England. Stuart had been sent to Aldro School, near Godalming in Surrey because it was reasonably near Granny who could act as a substitute mother, preparing clothes and visiting the school. Also her youngest son, Rowan, my uncle, had gone there many years before, so she had a good opinion of it.

These two choices for my brothers were to have enormous consequences for me too. I followed Stuart to Aldro in September 1946, the term after he left. And four years later I was to follow the departed Hugh and Stuart to Kings School Canterbury senior school which returned to its rightful home in Kent after its war evacuation to Cornwall. The location of these schools bore no relationship to where Mother was and only a little bearing on where Granny lived.

Aldro School stands in Shackleford Village, not far from Guildford. The main building and its many little outhouses, including an octagonal cider press built of brick and flint stone, have a sense of age and permanence without seeming to belong to a particular period. Beautiful playing fields surround most of the house with a lake and boathouse on the very far side.

When I arrived as a boarder on the cobbled driveway at the age of ten, this was my seventh school, which inevitably meant that I was under-educated and likely to be regarded as 'backward.' As I looked about me, other boys of my age seem to have had a more tranquil childhood and knew a lot more than I did, though where they could have been hiding from the war I will never know. Aldro was, and still is, an all boys' school and so soon after the war there were men on the staff who had recently returned from military service. They were always in evidence, ready to give conversation and encouragement to the boys and to play games with enthusiasm, even if they were not expert at hitting or kicking balls in the right direction.

The school was run by the extraordinary headmaster Mr. F. E. Hill and his ample and efficient wife Mrs. Hill. 'F.E.H,' as he was known, was red faced and could be fierce; he had very high moral standards and his belief in discipline always related to a strong Christianity. It was also apparent that he believed boys are best if you fill their days with masses of activity. He was like a Victorian Actor Manager, so his shows of fierce disapproval for wrong-doings were more like theatrical performances than admonishments from a grim headmaster. However, we were extremely wary of him. Small, war-torn boys were no match for his explosive personality. But because he was absolutely fair and just, and because he had a highly charged imagination, he commanded loyalty and respect from the boys and staff, who felt he cared about them in spite of his frightening manner. His dramatic talents were impressive when he read to us, toothpaste-smelling boys, before bed, in his study at night.

One dark winter's evening we were doing

'homework' in our respective classrooms. Mine at that time was called Russell Hall, a room I loved. It felt like a flag-stoned stable a few hundred yards from the main school building. To reach the main house from this classroom you had to go down a narrow, brick-paved passageway before crossing the drive. The master on duty in Russell Hall sent me on a short errand with a note to a teacher in the main house. When I came out again into the driveway to return to my classroom a dark figure barred my way. Was he a tramp? He stooped challengingly towards my small frame, like a bull about to charge. In a rough, husky voice he said:

'Where are you going?'

'Going back to my classroom.'

'No you're not!'

'But I've got to,' I replied nervously. They'll wonder where I am.'

'You're not going anywhere; do you hear me?'

I was alarmed by now and was wondering whether to run round him, or to retreat back into the school. But at this moment the tramp rose up to his full height and said, in the high, sing-song voice I recognised:

'Goodnight, Grainger.'

It was of course Mr. Hill practising a dramatic characterisation. Once he had done his performance all was well, and he probably thought I had handled the scene satisfactorily because, during a celebration evening at the end of the Christmas term, he had me playing Hamlet on the battlements in the opening scene of the play, confronting the ghost of the prince's father. Was the evening tramp scene my audition?

He directed us in snippets of Macbeth and in a full school play called 'They Made the Royal Arms' – about historical characters who, over the centuries, had contributed to the appearance of the Royal Coat of Arms. This wouldn't be of much interest today, but, after the war in Britain there was still a strong feeling of patriotism, also evident in many black and white films of the time. I was given the art job of painting lots of posters with shields and lions and unicorns to advertise the show, alongside an artist boy-genius called Bill Cobbett. Very occasionally there comes along a boy or girl who can just 'do it.' And Cobbett could certainly do drawing. I can imagine his drawing people when he was still in his pushchair. Alongside this prodigy I was a clumsy novice but he never made me feel anything but his companion.

The great strength of this school was in the number of activities on offer. Everyone could find something he was good at so each one developed some self-respect. There was no bullying that I ever saw; we were too busy being active. I involved myself with photography, bookbinding, athletics, diving, acting and reciting. I found I was good at .22 target-shooting with a rifle. We lay on sandbags aiming at targets at the far end of a greenhouse, with glass all around, so we had to be accurate.

But, before these opportunities could really start to help me, my rebellious spirit, which had started to show itself in Hove, had one last great explosion. I ran away from school with a boy called Radin – I didn't know his first name, we never used them at school.

The final friction between my parents which I had witnessed was worrying me. Father had visited me at Aldro soon after I arrived but he was strained and depressed and there was no close relationship between us, so I probably felt that I should find my way home and sort things out.

Miss Harries, our teacher, regularly held nature walks in Shackleford Woods near the school, so on one of these Radin and I detached ourselves. We reached Milford on foot but without any plans of what to do next, and without any money for fares, our options were limited. We lifted a few carrots to eat from a garden, making the owner angry, and climbed a tree like isolated monkeys to consider our position. Defeated, we walked back to school to face the consequences of our brief escape. Mr. Hill made us realise the selfishness of our action and how extremely worried we had made everyone, particularly poor Miss Harries, so, taking us one at a time to the dormitory, he beat us with six lashes of a cane, a very rare punishment at that school, only reserved for the most extreme offences.

Radin didn't return to Aldro the following term. It was said that he led me astray and I wouldn't have run away without his giving me the idea, but I have never agreed with that as a general theory in life. Whatever we do, where there is a free choice, we are responsible, however much pressure is put on us by somebody else. We can always say 'no.' I love a quote from the end of Tom Stoppard's play 'Rosencrantz and Guildenstern Are Dead:'

'There must have been a moment, at the beginning,

Dennis White at Aldro, 1949

when we could have said – no. But somehow we missed it.'

I have never resented the punishment I received

Dennis White became my form master and remained my friend for the remaining thirty-six years of his life. He was about twenty-four and I was ten when we met at Aldro, both of us arriving at the same time. He had lost the sight in one eye during army service in a tank. Looking at him, both eyes looked normal, so few people realised his disability. Like many war survivors he never referred to his experiences which I suspect were terrible, and it is extraordinary how enthusiastic and active he was with such impaired eyesight. For example, though not being in any way a sportsman himself, he was very keen on cricket, ran the Second XI and frequently umpired matches; this is difficult enough with two good eyes. The problems Dennis must have had never occurred to anybody because he never referred to them. He wanted to be regarded as normal. His great passion was for literature and the arts and because he loved poetry the boys soon took an interest in it too. We performed a dramatised version of the speech from Shakespeare's 'As You Like It,'

'All the world's a stage,
And all the men and women merely players.
They have their exits and their entrances,
And one man in his time plays many parts,
His acts being seven ages…'

Each one of us played a character from one of

Chris jumping over the artist William Cobbett,
Aldro, 1950

the ages, from schoolboy to old man, and for the performance in front of the whole school Dennis hired costumes from a firm in London at his own expense, while a real barrister's wig for the judge arrived in a cardboard box borrowed from a willing lawyer-parent.

Dennis was not always benign. His dreamy Mount Olympus could sometimes erupt into a volcano. Once, in the lovely old classroom, Russell Hall, he felt unappreciated and became angry at the class:

'I try to do so much to help you boys, but you do nothing I ask you to do.'

Then he walked out of the room, leaving us speechless and shocked. At a loss to know what to do next, I made a quick line drawing of his face from memory, moustache bristling, looking displeased.

On returning a little while later he caught sight of the drawing as I must have made a bad job of hiding it. Instead of disapproving of my little creation and punishing me, which would have been the reaction of most schoolmasters at that time, he took it, laughed at it, and showed it proudly to the class. He kept this small drawing for the rest of his life and sometimes brought it out of a drawer in his study to show me many years later.

Before I left we performed the whole of 'A Midsummer Night's Dream' to the rest of the school and to the village. His theory was that if young people are called upon to perform drama which is a little beyond their understanding it will raise them, rouse them and they will respond to the challenge. Also he knew they would never forget the experience.

Dennis White encouraged all my artistic interests: painting, music, theatre. In the holidays he took a small group of us to the Old Vic Theatre in London to see Shakespeare plays. He was keen on a vegetarian restaurant in Leicester Square run by a friendly Hungarian gentleman, always pleased to see us, and I liked the vegetables, or eggs, in cheese sauce. Later on in life Dennis introduced me to the delights of Italy, and he had an important influence on many other boys over two generations, encouraging them to discover aspects of life which they might never have enjoyed without his initial enthusiasm. Many years later I met a man called Hastings, one of two brothers. We had all been at Aldro at exactly the same time so I mentioned Dennis:

'Dennis White?' he said, 'Oh he was fantastic. My life just wouldn't have been the same without Dennis White.'

As Dennis felt the 'After Life' was how well people remembered you after you died, he would have been very pleased with these comments.

In January 1947 there was a famously cold winter; the Aldro lake froze over for the rest of the term and instead of having to play hockey or rugby we slid across the ice and played in the snow like figures in a Dutch painting. When it suddenly all melted in April, just before the end of term, Shackleford became awash under a deep flood.

The school was keen on music. I sang solos in the school choir and we went carol singing around the village before Christmas; a torch-lit, frosty, exciting experience. Because I had come to the school at a later age than most entrants, and in such a fragmented state, I was allowed to stay on there until I was fourteen while most boys left a year earlier. This extra time allowed me to achieve some of those lofty positions which mean a lot to a schoolboy but nothing at all to the world outside: I became a 'Squad Commander' and captain of shooting and even won a cup for diving – into the lake – which I never actually received because they hadn't quite bought the cup when I left.

Aldro had done a brilliant job with me; encouraging me to believe in myself; allowing me to discover things I was good at and giving me a vision that life is full of exciting and beautiful mysteries to be explored.

Meanwhile the family home had been moved from near the sea in Lansdown Place to a house high in the suburbs of Hove, called 'Dykelands.'

The Grainger brothers, 1950

SEVEN

The unpleasant separation of my parents had prevented their planning or discussing what was best for our education. Once the school course was set we each followed one another like a paper chase. Peter had been with me for a year at St. Christopher's, Hove, before I went to Aldro. He then followed me to Aldro before I went to King's School, Canterbury, where he ended up, after me, as a scholar, to be more academically successful than any of us. This school was not a good choice for me. It was a long way from Brighton and it offered none of the subjects I was most interested in. There was no art room – just a man who turned up on a bicycle on Saturday afternoons, who took a voluntary class for anyone in the school who might be interested. Before him there were some very poor art classes given by a man who had been gassed in the First World War who had few ideas and, with his breathing difficulties, was unable to keep any useful control of the pupils. I desperately needed something more dynamic than this.

Situated in the precincts of Canterbury cathedral, there was inevitably a lot of good music. Hugh and Stuart had both left the school together before I arrived. They had certainly not been happy and seemed to have gained very little from their time there; nevertheless I was sent to follow them without any discussion about whether this was the best choice for me.

Public schools are run on totally different lines from preparatory, or junior schools, or most of them

Hugh playing his drums in Dykelands garden, 1953

were in 1950. While the younger schools are staffed by adults who influence every area, the public school is largely run by youths – the senior pupils. At that time they had the authority to beat younger boys with a slipper, and could decide punishments without any reference to an adult. This gave them more power than their maturity could handle, so frequently it led to injustice and to resentment and an unsettled atmosphere among the younger pupils, like a farmyard where there is the rumour of a slaughterhouse. Selection to these powerful positions of authority seldom seemed to be based on a senior boy's wisdom or sense of justice to others; more on whether he had a good academic performance in the classroom – in which case he would swagger about in a purple gown carrying a black stick crowned with a silver knob; or if he had a heroic record on the playing field – a scorer of tries or a hitter of sixes. So it was a breeding ground for little tyrants. The staff, mostly male, were kept back, like indifferent stud animals, for inseminating knowledge in the classroom. Many of these masters had very good university degrees, outwardly signalled by the coloured and furry hoods that hung down the rear of their black gowns, as if clasped by a deflated supplicant. But unfortunately they had not been selected for their teaching ability and most of them lacked enthusiasm for the job. After the dedication I had found at Aldro this was a great disappointment to me. The few good teachers were allotted to the most able pupils, leaving the rest of us to do our best with very little help or encouragement.

King's School Wind Band, 1953
Showing Canterbury Cathedral. (Chris on the right.)

In the midst of this confusion a bizarre and dangerous event happened: I was walking in the quadrangle called The Mint Yard when I suddenly heard the snap of gunfire. Two bullets zipped past my head. Swinging round to look behind me I saw, up at a first floor window, the muzzles of two rifles pointing at me with two grinning faces above the guns. Two boys had raided a Canterbury gun store the night before and were testing their stolen goods on me as a joke target. Instead of the snipers being expelled from the school the whole episode was hushed up to avoid bad publicity in the national newspapers.

Soon after the gun theft there was a stabbing. During a class with the gassed art master one boy asked another to pass him a pencil eraser. When he refused he was stabbed with a penknife, the wound narrowly missing his kidney.

For years afterwards I wondered whether I had imagined these serious incidents, or perhaps I had created them in my own mind as a private revenge against the school. If I asked anyone about them they said they couldn't remember.

I was to discover how well they had been covered up thirty years later when I met John Corner, who had been a senior master at King's at the time of the criminal behaviour. He wrote and told me that both events had happened exactly as I remembered them. He had been personally instructed by the headmaster, Canon Shirley, to convince the Chief Constable of Kent that the whole matter would be better handled internally by the school. John Corner also told me that the parents of the dayboy who was stabbed said, after their son was taken to hospital:

'Oh well, I suppose we have to expect these things if we send our boy to public school.'

It was at this school I learnt to play the clarinet. The teacher of wind instruments, Paddy Purcell, was a very good clarinettist himself. He was jovial and kind and very good with the age group he was teaching, but my rebellious characteristics which had been so brilliantly tamed at Aldro were now returning in my teenage years. I was realising that I did not fit well into this place and the sooner I could leave it forever the happier I would be. I was sometimes absent from band practices which distressed Paddy as he was a military band expert and regarded reliability, quite rightly, as very important. As often happens when we are unhappy we do things which only make matters worse. I didn't turn up to sit my 'O' Level Latin exam paper. My logic seemed perfectly reasonable at that age; if I wasn't going to pass, what was the point of sitting there writing the exam paper. But I didn't take into account the stress I was causing to my teacher, Mr. Goodes. It just didn't occur to my limited, blinkered, teenage mind.

There was a proud moment to remember though. In the whole school of five hundred boys I was the only one sitting the Art 'O' Level exam. I did the best I could to teach myself the history of art syllabus which was one of the papers, and to learn to draw in the only limited way I knew. I sat in the huge exam hall all alone – The Parry Hall – and passed.

Because of Dennis White's fine early teaching I

had no difficulty with either of the English papers and another strength was Biology, simply because the master, Charlie Ward, had taken a little bit of trouble with me and tolerated my careful drawings of plants, circulation and digestive systems. Others did diagrams while I introduced shading which took longer, so I could have been criticised.

Writing this memory of childhood and my early youth has made me see how amazingly fortunate I was to have some magnificent person turn up in my life whenever there was a dark and difficult period. A guardian angel would show up each time I was lost. An angel doesn't need to have wings. So it was that, just as I was despairing of this brutish organisation called a Public School, John Corner, the senior master already mentioned, appeared. He was a language teacher, specialising in German who never actually taught me in class but was to offer me a steadying hand for a short while. He ran a Saturday evening literary club called The Walpole Society (Horace Walpole had evidently once been a pupil at the school.) A small group of us from different houses came together to read plays and stories in the kindly, civilised atmosphere of his room, low-lit by table lamps. After we had read some interesting stories by Somerset Maugham, and short plays by Terence Rattigan, Mr. Corner organised a short story competition which I won. At the time, of course, it felt like a big success because I was hungry for achievement, but really there were very few entries as our group was small. My story was about a pavement artist who accidentally lost a very valuable coin which

Chris, Stuart, Hugh and Peter at Dykelands, 1954

had been put into his hat by mistake. I hoped it would be published in the school magazine but this was blocked by my housemaster, Mr. Sopwith, who was also Head of English. I would have liked him to see me personally to explain the story's weaknesses, after all he only lived up the stairs, but instead he returned my script with a note written in his tiny classicist handwriting on a sheet of lined paper from a school exercise book, with strange affected abbreviations like shd. instead of should, and pd. instead of paid.

John Corner did his best for me with Sopwith but publication was not to be. I will always be grateful to him for believing in me during that final year of school.

Not everything was grim. At Aldro I had been the first warden of the new chapel which had been converted from a barn in my final year, so I was the first boy to ring the bell for a service, had read lessons and sung in the choir. By the time I was confirmed on the altar steps of Canterbury Cathedral I was well marinated in the traditions of the Church of England. A large group of us were prepared for confirmation by a noble friar with a grey beard in the crypt of the cathedral. For several days we were 'in retreat,' which meant we were not to talk to anyone.

The Archbishop of Canterbury at the time was Geoffrey Fisher who had the most wonderful voice, not loud or actorish but very spiritual, as if he was speaking from a position somewhere between here and Heaven, and he performed the laying-on-of-hands at our confirmation. Not long afterwards he officiated at the Coronation of Queen Elizabeth II and placed the crown on the Queen's head in Westminster Abbey. As far as I know the Queen was never told that he had laid hands on us first.

My first communion early the next morning, in the cathedral crypt, was a spiritual experience of great power, contained within ancient walls, with tall candles and colourful robes; very different from granny's scrubbed and well-hoovered church.

I made two great friendships at King's: Tom Osborne and Clive Graham who have remained friends ever since. Tom and I took an active interest in whatever we could, while Clive, slightly younger, oversaw and protected us both as if he was our kindly uncle. The three of us bought a small Adana printing press by mail order, complete with metal type. Tom and I printed letter headings and Christmas cards while Clive, the non-executive director, looked on with encouragement without getting his fingers dirty. Our printing enterprise was stopped by Mr. Sopwith, the housemaster, just as our sales figures were looking good, because some boy in charge of us – probably the Head of House – had told him that printing interfered with our homework. So the order came from Sopwith's Study (no sign of the man in person) that we were not to be involved in 'Trade,' and – as happens in a police state – all activity on the press must cease.

This was still the time in England when prisoners convicted of murder were hanged. There was a young man called Derek Bentley who, after a robbery, was sentenced to death for shooting a policeman when he had not done so; a young accomplice of sixteen had pulled the trigger but was too young to hang, so they decided to make an example of Bentley. We three friends felt this was so unjust – that a man was to be hanged, though innocent of a crime which carried the death sentence. So we rigged up a radio receiver under the floorboards of the dormitory by taking unseen wires up through the house, from a radio downstairs, so that we could listen to the early morning news and observe a secret vigil of sympathy at the exact time when the hanging was carried out.

The night before I finally left school Clive and I undertook a daring adventure. After dark we made our way down the Norman Staircase from the dormitory, across the short grass of the precincts, hiding between big white marquees, which stood like canvas temples to sparkling wine after Parents' Day, and climbed up some builders' scaffolding onto the cathedral roof. We picked our pathway through this normally unseen world of gulleys and buttresses with great care, knowing we could be seen in the floodlights at any moment. After a while we came to a little door which opened onto a spiral staircase leading down to another door. We opened this very slowly. It revealed the gigantic dark inside of the cathedral. The effigy of The Black Prince lay on his tomb in front of us while the echo of the opened door still rang through the vacuous darkness. A cathedral interior in daytime, lit up, with lots of people, can be very pleasant, but all alone at night in its vast blackness with only one way of escape is a very different experience, so we decided this was enough and ran back to the house the way we had come, without anyone knowing we had been missing.

Having bought the other two shares from my friends I took the Adana printing press home with me and left school aged seventeen at the end of the summer term in 1953.

In September I started at Brighton College of Arts and Crafts. When I walked through its doors for the first time, experiencing the exciting smell of distempered walls and linseed oil, and seeing the students, male and female, advancing towards different rooms where they were going to create things, I knew without doubt that this was where I belonged at last. After all those countless boys' schools I could now work alongside girls and that was an exciting study in itself. We could all learn to draw and paint and design and letter. We could make a difference to our surroundings with lines and forms and colours.

When we are children every move, every school and every condition at home or away is decided by others. When we leave school at last we begin to have the right to decide where we go, where we work and in what kind of atmosphere we live; this is the difference between the child and the man. After my own childhood this new found freedom felt liberating; as if I had been released from a long confinement in a land full of restrictions, and I have valued that freedom ever since.

CHRIS ROWAN GRAINGER

Studied at Brighton College of Art, Farnham School of Art and the Bristol Old Vic Theatre School. He appeared in several plays with the Bristol Old Vic Company before deciding to concentrate on the visual arts. He travelled extensively in Italy, studying the early frescoes, and has had twelve one man exhibitions of his paintings and sculptures in London and elsewhere. His work has been shown in many mixed exhibitions including the Royal Academy and The London Group, and is represented in private collections in Britain, Europe and the USA.

He has been involved in the writing of five published books, some of them containing reproductions of his paintings:

The Gate
The Divine Springtime
Colours Rising
Talking Amongst Myself
Bombs at Bedtime

www.ingramcontent.com/pod-product-compliance
Lightning Source LLC
Chambersburg PA
CBHW032131090426
42743CB00007B/566